Looking at the Birds

Heather Hammonds

Contents

Rigby®

A Harcourt Achieve Imprint

www.Rigby.com

1-800-531-5015

The Park

I went to the park
with my grandpa.
We went to the park
to look at the birds.

We had fun
looking at the birds!

By a Tree

We hid by a tree.

We sat very still.

Some little birds

came down on the grass.

The little birds

did not see us.

sparrows

A Bird Book

Grandpa had a **bird book**.
He helped me read
his book.

I saw little birds like this
in Grandpa's bird book.

sparrows

A Bird's Nest

We saw a nest in a tree.

We saw some baby birds

in the nest.

blackbirds

The mother bird
had some food
for the baby birds!

Hungry Birds

We saw some hungry birds.

Grandpa had some **seeds**

for the hungry birds.

The birds stayed by us.

They did not fly away.

pigeons

In the Pond

We went to the pond at the park.

We saw some birds swimming in the pond.

ducks

13

My Bird

I went home with Grandpa.

I have a little bird
at home.

It is green and yellow.
It is my pet!

parakeet

Glossary

bird book

seeds